PowerDown teachers' booklet

Contents

How to use the *PowerDown* toolkit

This toolkit is a cross-curricular resource for primary schools focusing on how energy use is linked to climate change.

A short PowerPoint slideshow is included on the *PowerDown* DVD-Rom to help explain how to use the toolkit and is ideal for use in inset sessions and teacher training.

PowerDown enables learners to investigate energy use at home and in their school, and how this is linked to extreme weather events thousands of miles away. The growing impacts of climate change are brought to life through stories from children in different parts of the world.

'Learner-centred action' lies at the heart of *PowerDown*. By studying some of the local, national and global solutions to climate change, learners are encouraged to discuss, plan and create their own climate change solutions.

This booklet contains lesson ideas, photocopiable activity sheets and further information.

The lesson ideas grid shows how the toolkit can form the basis of ten lessons. Each lesson has clear curriculum links and learning outcomes.

Lesson plans follow a simple, three-step approach: learn, investigate, act. Photo cards, activity sheets or video footage accompany each step.

This toolkit offers:

- ➡ real and relevant learning – connecting learning to the world beyond the classroom
- ➡ clear learning outcomes – relating particularly to science, geography and citizenship
- ➡ learner-centred activities – supporting personal, learning and thinking skills
- ➡ a compelling learning experience – encouraging confident and responsible learners
- ➡ cross-curricular lesson ideas – supporting education for sustainable development and the global dimension.

Photo cards are designed for pupils to read in groups or pairs. They are divided into Learn and Solutions photo cards. They are colour coded for ease of use:

- blue cards (1-3) give learners an introduction to the causes and impacts of climate change
- orange cards (4-10) are stories showing the impact of climate change on people and places
- red cards (11-15) investigate how energy is used at school and in the home
- green cards (16-22) highlight some of the solutions to slowing climate change and are designed to inspire learners' own ideas.

Learn photo cards

1. *Introduction: what is climate change?*
2. *Introduction: why is the earth getting hotter?*
3. *Introduction: how is climate change affecting our world?*
4. *Climate change around the world: Mahidul's story, Bangladesh*
5. *Climate change around the world: Fatima's story, India*
6. *Climate change around the world: Zakir's story, India*
7. *Climate change around the world: Biblop's story, Bangladesh*
8. *Climate change around the world: Abbas' story, India*
9. *Climate change around the world: Sophia's story, Tanzania*
10. *Climate change around the world: the Amazon rainforest story*
11. *Climate change and energy use: the big picture*
12. *Climate change and energy use: heat at school*
13. *Climate change and energy use: electricity at school*
14. *Climate change and energy use: energy loss at home*
15. *Climate change and energy use: transport*

Solutions photo cards

16. *Climate change solutions: global solutions*
17. *Climate change solutions: people power*
18. *Climate change solutions: Good Energy*
19. *Climate change solutions: Hamsey Green junior school, England*
20. *Climate change solutions: Ashley Church of England primary school, England*
21. *Climate change solutions: St Martin at Shouldham CEVA primary school, England*
22. *Climate change solutions: Karchua Bori school, India*

PowerDown lesson ideas

Learn

These activities are designed to be used alongside the Learn photo cards 1-15, *Be the solution* trigger film and Activity sheets 1-6. Learners may also find the *Keywords information sheet* helpful.

Activity	Curriculum links	Key questions and ideas	Teaching and learning	Resources
Mind mapping Keywords **Learning journey** This is what I already know This is what I want to know This is what I've found out	**KS2 geography:** – observe and record key features – use secondary sources of information – study an environmental issue – use appropriate geographical vocabulary. **KS2 citizenship:** – to research, discuss and debate topical issues, problems and events.	What do we already know about climate change? What would we like to know? What have we learnt so far?	**Part one** What words come into your mind when you think of climate change? Write as many as you can on your *mind map* sheet. **Part two** Share keywords. Write them as sentences under 'This is what I already know' on your *learning journey* sheet. What else would you like to find out? Add these thoughts to the *my learning journey* sheet under 'This is what I want to find out'. Now watch the *Be the solution* trigger film. **Part three** What have you learnt from the film? Anything you didn't already know? If so, add this to the *my learning journey* sheet under 'This is what I have learned'.	*Climate change: my mind map* (Activity sheet 1) *Climate change: my learning journey* (Activity sheet 2) *Be the solution* (*PowerDown* DVD-Rom) *Keywords information sheet*

Activity	Curriculum links	Key questions and ideas	Teaching and learning	Resources
Photo investigation What I see What I've found out What I want to say	**KS2 geography:** – ask geographical questions – identify how and why places change in terms of climate, and how and why they may change in the future. **KS2 English:** – draw on images to obtain meaning – ask relevant questions to clarify, extend and follow up ideas – use word classes, including verbs, adjectives. **KS2 science SC1:** – pupils should be taught that science is about thinking creatively to... establish links between causes and effects. **KS2 citizenship:** – to talk and write about their opinions, and explain their views, on issues that affect themselves and society.	What is climate change? Why is the earth getting hotter? How is our climate changing? How is climate change affecting people now? How might it affect people and places in the future?	**Part one** Use an interactive whiteboard/projector to show Learn photo cards 1-3 to the whole class. What do you think each picture/graphic shows? What has it got to do with climate change? Read the back of the cards. What's the most important thing you've learnt about climate change now/in the future? **Part two** Divide learn photo cards 4-10 among pupils. Place each photo in the centre of a large piece of paper. Place cut-out shapes from the *photo investigation* sheet around it. What is happening in your picture? What do you think it has to do with climate change? Complete 'What I see'. Read the back of your card. What have you learnt about the picture/about climate change? Complete 'What I've found out'. What is the most important thing you want to tell the class about this picture? Complete 'What I want to say'. **Part three** Each group shows their photo to the class and feeds back 'What I want to say'. Extended activity – learners could add more thoughts to their *my learning journey* sheet 'This is what I have learned'.	Learn photo cards – introduction: (digital versions on DVD-Rom) 1. *What is climate change?* 2. *Why is the earth getting hotter?* 3. *How is climate change affecting our world?* Learn photo cards – climate change around the world: 4. *Mahidul's story, Bangladesh* 5. *Fatima's story, India* 6. *Zakir's story, India* 7. *Biblop's story, Bangladesh* 8. *Abbas' story, India* 9. *Sophia's story, Tanzania* 10. *The Amazon rainforest story* *Climate change: photo investigation* (Activity sheet 3)

Activity	Curriculum links	Key questions and ideas	Teaching and learning	Resources
Energy use inquiry My notes: how are we wasting energy? My ideas: how could we waste less energy?	**KS2 science SC1** – pupils should be taught that science is about thinking creatively to... establish links between causes and effects. **KS2 geography:** – use secondary sources of information – study an environmental issue – use appropriate geographical vocabulary – decision-making skills, eg deciding what measures are needed to reduce energy.	Where does our energy come from? What is a fossil fuel? What is energy used for? What has energy use/waste got to do with climate change? What uses/wastes the most energy in our schools and homes?	**Part one** Whole class: use interactive whiteboard/projector to show photo card 11. Read and discuss: What do we use energy for? (heat, transport, power) What is a fossil fuel? (oil, coal, gas) What do fossil fuels release when they are burned? (carbon dioxide) **Part two** Divide photo cards 12-15 among the class. Each group reads each card for 5 minutes; writes notes on their *energy use inquiry* sheet for five minutes; then swaps cards with another group. **Part three** How are we wasting energy? How could we waste less energy? Each group feeds back their findings/ideas to whole class.	Learn photo card (digital version on DVD-Rom) – climate change and energy use: 11. *The big picture* Learn photo cards – climate change and energy use: 12. *Heat at school* 13. *Electricity at school* 14. *Energy loss at home* 15. *Transport* *Energy use inquiry* (Activity sheet 4)

Activity	Curriculum links	Key questions and ideas	Teaching and learning	Resources
Making the connections	**KS2 science:** – know that science is about thinking creatively to try to explain how living and non-living things work, and to establish links between causes and effects – understand ways in which living things and the environment need protection. **KS2 geography:** – analyse evidence and draw conclusions – recognise and explain how people can cause changes in places and environments.	Why is the earth getting hotter? What type of weather might we expect as the earth gets hotter? What has using energy got to do with this?	**Part one** Revisit pupils' *learning journey* sheets. Have we learnt anything else about climate change? Share ideas/add to sheets. **Part two** Cut out the boxes on *making the connections* activity sheet. Put them in order to help explain how turning on a light switch is connected to climate change. This could be presented in diagram form or as a written news article to help other people make the connections. **Part three** What has switching on a light got to do with climate change? Pupils take turns to talk for 30 seconds.	*Climate change: my learning journey* (Activity sheet 2) *Climate change: making the connections* (Activity sheet 5)

Activity	Curriculum links	Key questions and ideas	Teaching and learning	Resources
Adapting to climate change	**KS2 design and technology:** – generate ideas for products, thinking about who will use them and what they will be used for, using information from a range of sources including ICT – recognise that the quality of a product depends on how well it meets social, economic and environmental considerations. **KS2 geography:** – recognise how people can improve the environment, and how decisions about places and environments affect the quality of people's lives.	How is climate change affecting people living in Bangladesh? How are some people in Bangladesh adapting to living with climate change? What can we learn from people in Bangladesh?	**Part one** Read the *build a Bangladeshi house* activity sheet and explain the instructions (as below). **Part two** 1. Cut up the boxes and the titles. Read the sentences in each box and match them to each title. 2. Take a big piece of paper. Draw a picture of a Bangladeshi house in the middle. 3. Paste the boxes and titles around your house. 4. Draw arrows connecting the boxes to the right places. **Part three** Consider how and why this house is flood-resistant and sustainable. Design your own flood-resistant house using recycled materials.	*Build a Bangladeshi house* (Activity sheet 6)

Investigate

This activity is designed to be used alongside Activity sheet 7. Learn photo cards 11-15 will also complement this activity.

Activity	Curriculum links	Key questions and ideas	Teaching and learning	Resources
Stop the energy thieves	**KS2 geography:** – recognise how people can improve or damage the environment, and how decisions about places and environments affect the future quality of people's lives – decision-making skills, eg deciding what measures are needed to reduce energy. **KS2 citizenship:** – to talk and write about their opinions, and explain their views, on issues that affect themselves and society.	What is wasting energy at school and at home? Are these energy thieves the same or different at home and at school? How can we keep these energy thieves under control?	**Part one** Re-cap on learners' *energy use inquiry*. Can you remember what we found out about energy and how we sometimes waste it? **Part two** In pairs/groups learners read the *stop the energy thieves* activity sheet. 1. Make a list of all the energy thieves at home and/or school. 2. How can you keep them under control? Share and write your ideas. **Part three** Design a 'Stop the energy thieves' poster to raise awareness among other classes.	*Stop the energy thieves* (Activity sheet 7)

Act

These activities are designed to be used alongside the Solutions photo cards. The photo cards introduce some of the local, national and global solutions to slowing down climate change. They include 'top tips' from three UK primary schools – designed to give learners some inspiring examples of what might work within a school and to act as a springboard for their own ideas. Learners may also find the *keywords information sheet* helpful. The *Assam slideshow* on the *PowerDown* DVD-Rom explains how one school in India is adapting to the threat of flooding.

Activity	Curriculum links	Key questions and ideas	Teaching and learning	Resources
Action card game	**KS2 geography:** – decision-making skills, eg deciding what measures are needed to reduce energy – recognise how and why people may seek to manage environments sustainably, and to identify opportunities for their own involvement. **KS2 PSHE and citizenship:** – take responsibility for planning and looking after the school environment – to face new challenges positively by collecting information, looking for help, making responsible choices and taking action.	There are many ways to *PowerDown* and make a difference. What actions can be taken to reduce energy use?	**Part one** Cut up the cards on the *action card game* activity sheet. There are two blank cards for learners to write in their own suggestions. If you come up with more than two ideas, replace a card. **Part two** Arrange the cards in a diamond pattern. Put the most preferred action at the top of the diamond and the least preferred action at the bottom of the diamond etc. **Part three** Consider which ones are the easiest actions to do; which could have the most impact.	*Action card game* (Activity sheet 8)

Activity	Curriculum links	Key questions and ideas	Teaching and learning	Resources
Which action?/Vote with your feet	**KS2 English:** – speaking and listening – talk effectively as members of a group. **KS2 citizenship:** – take responsibility – feel positive about themselves – participate – make real choices and decisions. **KS2 geography:** – decision-making skills, eg deciding what measures are needed to reduce energy.	Which action is the best? The *which action?* matrix helps learners to consider which action might be the most effective and successful. Using the matrix they are asked to consider: How easy will it be to carry out this action? What will we need? Who can help us? How many people could our action reach? If learners cannot reach a consensus then they can 'vote with their feet'!	**Part one** Give groups of learners the *which action?* activity sheet. Ask them to write their three most popular actions in the left-hand columns. **Part two** Discuss and answer the following questions about each action: – How easy is it to do? – What will we need (eg space, equipment)? – Who can help us? – How many people will see our idea? As a group agree the best action and the reasons for your decision. **Part three** Whole class feedback. Each group outlines their chosen action and why it is 'the best action to do'. The class then votes on the best overall action. If they cannot decide use 'vote with your feet' as follows: write each group's action on a piece of paper. Place each one in a different corner of the room. When you call "vote with your feet", pupils run to the corner with their favourite action.	*Which action?* (Activity sheet 9)

Activity	Curriculum links	Key questions and ideas	Teaching and learning	Resources
Action tree	**KS2 geography:** – recognise how and why people may seek to manage environments sustainably, and to identify opportunities for their own involvement. **KS2 citizenship:** – take responsibility for planning and looking after the school environment – to face new challenges positively by collecting information, looking for help, making responsible choices, and taking action.	The *action tree* is a creative tool. It helps learners plan their action creatively while considering the following: What do we want to achieve? What tools do we need to carry out our action? What tasks need to be done? Who will carry out each task? Who else can help us? Learners could do a shared class tree for display, or smaller trees in groups.	**Part one** Decide on an action to take, or use the one agreed in the *which action?* activity. **Part two** Draw your *Action tree* using the activity sheet as a guide. Trunk: our action. Roots: tools or resources we need. Branches: tasks to carry out. Leaves: people who will carry out each task. Fruit: what we want to achieve. Worms: helpers. **Part three** Take your action!	*Action tree* (Activity sheet 10)

Activity	Curriculum links	Key questions and ideas	Teaching and learning	Resources
Reflections	**KS2 citizenship:** – to recognise their worth as individuals by identifying positive things about themselves and their achievements, seeing their mistakes, making amends and setting personal goals. **KS2 English:** – speaking and listening – explaining, reporting, evaluating.	**Changing me** What did you enjoy most? Did you learn any new skills? Has this changed the way you might think or behave? **Working together** How did we work together? Which tasks did you enjoy the most? Were you happy with the decisions your group made? **Making a difference** Have we made a difference? How do we know? What was our greatest success? **Next time** What worked well/not so well? What was the most difficult thing you did? Is there anything you would do differently next time?	**Part one** Consider your action. What worked well, and what would you do differently next time? **Part two** Use one of the *reflections* activity sheets to describe what difference the action made, and the evidence you have to show this. **Part three** Share your reflections with the class. What was the impact on you/your school /the world?	*Reflections* (Activity sheet 11)

Climate change: my mind map

Activity sheet 1

Climate change: my learning journey

Activity sheet 2

This is what I already know	This is what I want to find out	This is what I have learned

Climate change: photo investigation

Activity sheet 3

Energy use inquiry

How are we wasting energy? My notes...

Information about heat	Information about electricity	Information about transport	Other information

How could we waste less energy? My ideas...

Climate change: making the connections

Cut out the boxes and put them in order to help explain how turning on a light switch is connected to flooding for people living near rivers and the sea.

The earth warms up causing global warming, leading to climate change.

Most power stations make electricity by burning coal, oil and natural gas.

When river and sea levels rise, people living nearby get flooded.

Carbon dioxide (CO_2) is a gas found in the atmosphere around our planet. It helps form an invisible blanket that keeps the earth warm by trapping heat.

Warmer weather is causing more rain and stronger storms. Heavy rain causes river and sea levels to rise.

Lights use electricity which is supplied by power stations.

Land ice and glaciers melt and flow into rivers and seas, adding to rising water levels.

The more carbon dioxide (CO_2) we produce, the more heat gets trapped in the atmosphere.

Warmer weather also causes sea temperatures to rise. The water molecules expand (get bigger) adding to rising sea levels.

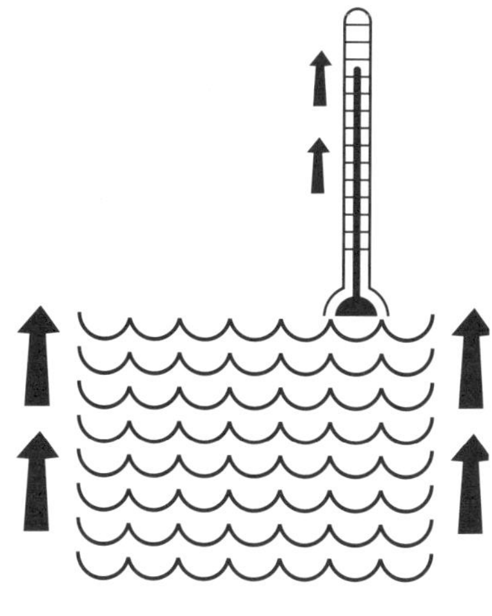

Burning oil, coal and natural gas creates carbon dioxide (CO_2). This goes into the air and some of it stays there.

The 'invisible blanket' works by trapping heat. Heat comes from the sun. It bounces off the earth but gets trapped by the 'blanket'.

Build a Bangladeshi house

Activity sheet 6

In 2007 flooding damaged four million homes in Bangladesh. More floods and stronger storms are likely as our climate changes. Building 'flood-resistant' houses will be very important. Can you draw the house below?

Can you match the text boxes to the titles? Cut out the boxes and titles. Now paste the matched boxes and titles around your house. Draw arrows connecting the boxes to the right places.

You will find me on each side of the house. I hold up the roof and provide protection from wind and rain. I am made from the fibre of a plant called jute. Jute is grown in Bangladesh. It is cheap, strong and 100% bio-degradable and recyclable.

I support the house and make it rigid and strong. I am made from a very tall, light and strong plant with hollow stalks. It is grown in Bangladesh and is the fastest growing woody plant in the world.

I provide protection from heavy rain. I am made using bamboo or corrugated iron. I keep the rain out.

I raise the house up. I am made from soil, a little cement and some stone and bricks. I need to be strong enough and high enough to withstand many floods. I should be raised at least 30cm above the ground.

Grow me around your house. I 'drink up' flood water and also hold onto the soil. Banana and bamboo varieties are best.

Titles:

plinth	bamboo frame	walls	roof	plants

Stop the energy thieves

Activity sheet 7

Electrical appliances – switch them off!

TVs, DVD players, PlayStations, Xboxes, Wiis, phone chargers, computers, projectors, electronic whiteboards – all eat lots of energy in 'standby mode'. A photocopier left on overnight uses enough energy to produce over 1,500 copies.

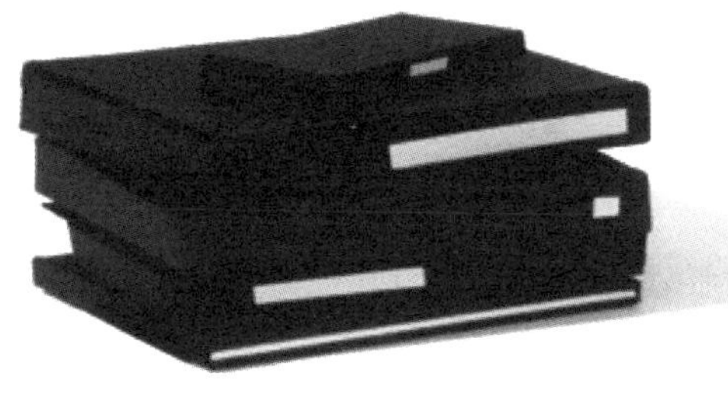

Radiators – turn down the heat!

Keep your thermostat at 18-20°C. Put a jumper on if you are cold.

Lights – do you really need them on?

Switch off lights when you leave a room. Traditional light bulbs waste 90% of the electricity they use as heat. Energy saving light bulbs last around 10 times longer – switching just one bulb could save 26 kilograms of carbon dioxide a year!

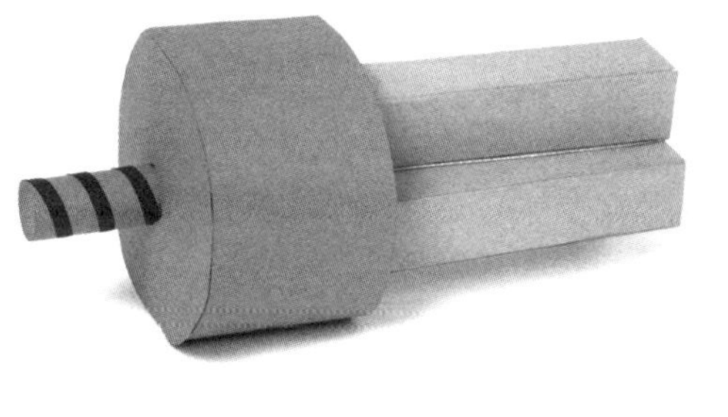

Windows and doors – keep them closed!

When you leave doors or windows open, and radiators on, heat escapes through the open spaces. Your radiators will have to use more energy to heat your school or home. What a waste!

1. Can you spot any of these energy thieves at home or at school?
2. How can you keep them under control?
3. Design a 'Stop the energy thieves' poster for other classes to look at.

Action card game

Activity sheet 8

Read the following suggestions for action and decide which one is the best for you to do. Two cards have been left blank for you to add your own suggestions.

The best action is to get parents, carers and the rest of the school involved by making some *PowerDown* posters to display around the school.

The best action is to ask people to act as *PowerDown* monitors for their class. Their job will be to make sure that energy does not get wasted around the school.

The best action is to ask a guest speaker into the school to explain more about climate change and what more we can do to *PowerDown*.

The best action is to write to our MP or ask him/her into school to explain what the government is doing to *PowerDown* and tackle climate change.

The best action is to write to the local papers and let them know about what our school is doing to *PowerDown*.

The best action is to organise a *PowerDown* day at school. We could make sure everyone makes a special effort to save energy on that day.

The best action is to organise a *PowerDown* competition and award prizes for the person who saves the most energy or comes up with the best idea.

The best action is:
(put your own idea here)

The best action is:
(put your own idea here)

Which action?

Our action ideas	**How easy is it to do?** 1 (easy) – 10 (hard)	**What will we need?** (space, equipment)	**Who can help us?**	**How many people will see our idea?**
Eg: organise a *PowerDown* competition with prizes for the class who saves most energy!	3	Eg: prizes, posters, assembly, judges	Eg: class, teacher, headteacher	Eg: whole school, parents
1.				
2.				
3.				

Action tree

Activity sheet 10

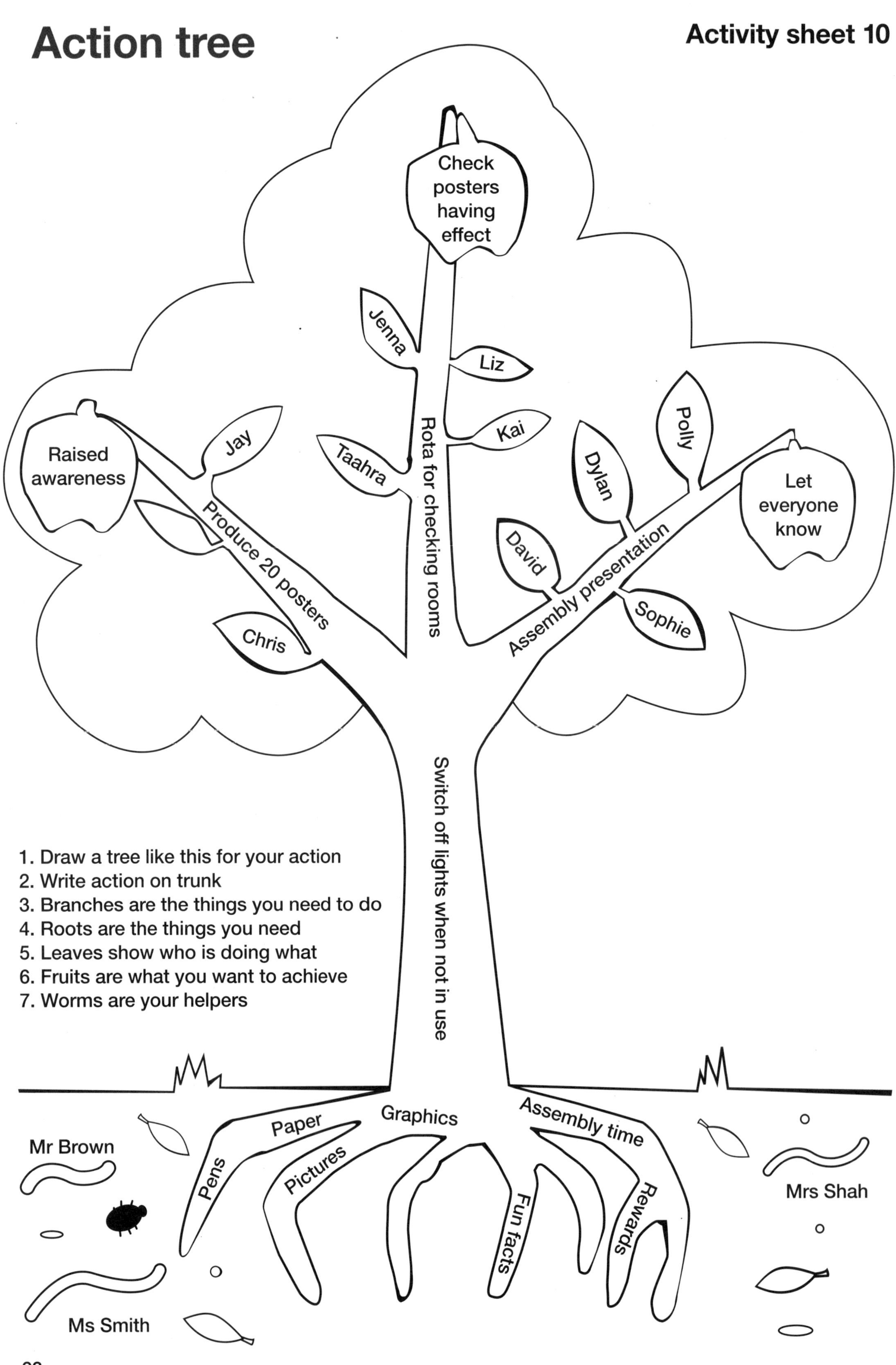

1. Draw a tree like this for your action
2. Write action on trunk
3. Branches are the things you need to do
4. Roots are the things you need
5. Leaves show who is doing what
6. Fruits are what you want to achieve
7. Worms are your helpers

Reflections

Changing me

What did you enjoy most?

Did you learn any new skills?

Has this changed the way you might think or behave?

Working together

How did we work together?

Which tasks did you enjoy the most?

Were you happy with the decisions your group made?

Our action

____

____

Making a difference

Have we made a difference?

How do we know?

What was our greatest success?

Next time

What worked well/not so well?

What was the most difficult thing you did?

Is there anything you would do differently next time?

Keywords information sheet

carbon dioxide (CO_2)

An 'invisible gas' in the air around us which makes up about 0.4% of the atmosphere. It is released when fuels like coal, oil and gas are burnt. It is also used by plants to capture and store energy.

climate

The average weather conditions over a long period of time (30-50 years).

drought

A long period without rain when crops cannot grow.

extinct

No longer living or existing, eg dinosaurs are extinct. Of all species that have ever lived, probably more than 90% are now extinct.

flood

When the water level temporarily rises and spills over onto land that is normally dry.

fossil fuels

Coal, oil and gas. Forms of energy created from fossilised plants, trees and creatures buried deep beneath the seabed millions of years ago.

global warming

An average increase in the Earth's temperature, which in turn causes changes in climate.

greenhouse gas

A gas (such as carbon dioxide) which forms a natural, invisible 'blanket' around the earth, keeping it warm.

heatwave

A period of unnaturally hot weather.

insulator

A material or object that doesn't let heat pass through it easily. Wool, plastic and rubber are good insulators because they keep heat in. You can slow down the speed at which heat escapes by using an insulator.

weather

The day-to-day condition of our atmosphere on a particular day, for example, how warm, cold, dry or wet each day is. Climate is what you 'expect' (eg warm summers) and weather is what you 'get' (eg rain).

Photo captions

Learn photo cards

1. What is climate change?
Aftermath of Hurricane Stan, Mexico, October 2005. 650mm of rain fell in a short period of time damaging roads and houses and cutting off communities from food supplies.

2. Why is the earth getting hotter?
Amazon drought, Brazil, October 2005. A horse crossing a dried up lake during one of the worst droughts ever recorded in the Amazon region.

3. How is climate change affecting our world?
Map showing what scientists think could happen if the world heats up by 3-5°C

4. Mahidul's story, Bangladesh
Mahidul, aged 11, fishing on the Brahmaputra river near his home in Char Jattrapur, northern Bangladesh.

5. Fatima's story, India
Fatima Begum, aged 7, from Karchua Bori village, Lower Assam, India, sits on a chang: an improvised raised platform used to escape the flood waters that entered her family's home.

6. Zakir's story, India
Zakir Hussain, aged 7, from Karchua Bori village, Lower Assam in northeast India.

7. Biblop's story, Bangladesh
Biplop, aged 11, at the shop he has worked in for the past two years. The shop is situated 14 miles from his family.

8. Abbas' story, India
Abbas Ali, aged 11, from Karchua Bori village, Lower Assam in northeast India.

9. Sophia's story, Tanzania
Sophia Larumbe, aged 13, from Arusha, Tanzania, walking donkeys to the river to collect water.

10. The Amazon rainforest story
Aerial view of the Amazon rainforest photographed during a flight from Alta Floresta to Santarem.

11. Climate change and energy use: the big picture
A pie chart showing how UK energy usage is split between heat, transport and electricity.

12. Heat at school
A school boiler. Most school boilers run off fossil fuels. However, this primary school boiler uses wood pellets which are effectively carbon neutral. This is because trees and plants absorb carbon dioxide when they grow and then emit that same amount of carbon dioxide when they're burnt.

13. Electrics at school
Year 9 pupil Paul from Langdon school, wondering why lights, PCs and monitors have been left on in an empty classroom.

14. Energy loss at home
This energy meter is a useful gadget for checking how much energy is being used in the home every day.

15. Transport
An aeroplane flying over a residential area in west London. Air travel is the UK's fastest growing source of carbon emissions.

Solutions photo cards

16. Global solutions
Visual representation of comparative resource usage between the USA, UK, India and Africa.

17. People power
Thousands of people make a big 'NO' in an anti Heathrow airport expansion protest.

18. Good Energy
A herdsman drives his sheep through the He Lan Shan wind farm in China.

19. Hamsey Green school
A walking bus. Children from Hamsey Green junior school walk to school.

20. Ashley Church or England primary school
PV solar panels on the roof of Ashley Church of England school collect sunlight and convert it into electricity.

21. St Martin at Shouldham school
A pupil from St Martin at Shouldham CEVA primary school explaining how pupils and staff are working together to save energy.

22. Karchua Bori school
In the village of Borbori, Assam, India, a volunteer demonstrates how empty bottles can be used to make a life jacket.

Brain-teaser answers and sources of information

Brain-teaser answers

Learn card 13:
1. £20 x 10 computers = £200
2. £20 x 10 computers x 30,000
UK schools = £6 million

Learn card 15:
Rail vs Air

Current CO_2 emissions per day = 6,000kg
(train 30 x 35 = 1,050) + (plane 30 x 165 = 4,950)

Effect from stopping flights between London and Manchester
10 extra trains needed
Total daily CO_2 savings = 4,600kg (6,000 air/rail) – (40 x 35 = 1,400 rail only)
Annual CO_2 savings = 1,679,000kg
(daily savings x 365, thirty flights per day is roughly the annual average)

Sources of information

Climate change: overview, causes and effects

'Climate change from the BBC weather centre'
www.bbc.co.uk/climate/evidence/extreme.shtml

'Humans blamed for climate change'
– IPPC report
http://news.bbc.co.uk/1/hi/sci/tech/6321351.stm

'At a glance: The Stern Review'
http://news.bbc.co.uk/1/hi/business/6098362.stm

'Global meltdown: scientists isolate areas most at risk of climate change'
www.guardian.co.uk/environment/2008/feb/05/climatechange

'Climate change: a quick guide'
www.direct.gov.uk/en/Environmentandgreenerliving/Thewiderenvironment/Climatechange/index.htm

'One planet – sustainable development'
www.wwflearning.org.uk/oneplanetschools/

Energy use and energy saving

'Your personal guide to saving the planet'
www.greenpeace.org.uk/blog/climate/your-personal-guide-to-helping-save-the-climate

'Energy benchmarking for schools'
– The Carbon Trust
http://217.10.129.104/energy_benchmarking/schools/download.asp

'Energy saving tips'
www.energysavingtrust.org.uk

'EfficienCity: a virtual, climate friendly city'
www.greenpeace.org.uk/efficiencity

Global footprints/carbon calculating

'The carbon gym – carbon calculating from the Centre for Alternative Technology'
www.cat.org.uk/carbongym

Deforestation and climate change

www.greenpeace.org.uk/forests/climate-change

www.independent.co.uk/environment/climate-change/deforestation-the-hidden-cause-of-global-warming-448734.html

Adapting to climate change

'Flood-resistant housing: adapting to climate change in Bangladesh'
http://practicalaction.org/?id=flood-resistant_housing

DN 32
FIG 500
KSM Stoker
Tlf. 97761072
STOP OXY21%
TEMP 026C PRG1
STOP START
SNEGL
MENU
OPSTART

Climate change and energy use: heat at school

In schools we spend more money on heating and producing hot water than anything else.

Stop heat and water waste!

Heat loves escaping from school buildings. It gets out of windows, doors and roofs. If you leave windows or doors open and radiators on, then heat will escape through the open spaces. Your poor radiators have to work extra hard, using more energy to heat your school!

"I can lose half my heat through walls and roofs. Help me stop heat escaping from my boilers, pipes and tanks. Please insulate me!"

Taps are very good at dripping if they are not turned off properly. This wastes lots of water and energy, especially the hot tap; hot water wastes more energy than cold, as it needs to be heated up.

"People love me when I'm nice and hot – but be careful how you use me. I waste lots of energy when you leave me running or dripping."

Top tip: how to save heat

- 18-20°C is an ideal room temperature.
- Check out the temperature in your classroom. Is it 18-20°C?
- No? Then find out who is in charge of controlling the temperature in your school.
- Ask them to keep the thermostat between 18-20°C.
- You could explain that reducing your room temperature by 1°C could cut heating bills by up to 10%, as well as saving precious energy!

What's in the picture on the front of this card?

Photo (front): Kristian Buus/ActionAid

COLECTIV

Introduction: what is climate change?

Planet Earth is around 4.5 billion years old.

During its lifetime, the Earth's temperature has changed many times, altering the planet's climate. These changes happen naturally and have been caused by changes in the amount of energy our planet gets from the sun, or events such as volcanic eruptions.

Photo: Corbis/Getty Images

This photo is a satellite image of Earth from space showing Africa and the Middle East.

When people talk about 'climate change' today, they are talking about changes that are happening in addition to this.
The change people are talking about is man-made and links back to the time when coal was first used to power industry.

Changes in the global temperature are a combination of natural events and man-made climate change. Sometimes both factors will cause global temperatures to increase. Sometimes natural events may cool the planet a little and mask or hide the effects of man-made climate change. However, man-made climate change is increasing and the Earth is getting hotter. Nine of the hottest years on the planet happened between 1997 and 2007.

As our planet gets warmer, the weather all over the Earth will change becoming less predictable. For example, it may not rain at all in places where people are expecting it, and it could rain too much in places where they are not expecting it.

The weather is likely to be more extreme, leading to droughts, floods, heatwaves and stronger storms.

There is little we can do about changes in the climate that happen naturally, like volcanoes, but we can slow down man-made climate change. There are lots of ways to help to keep the planet cool. Check out the *PowerDown* solutions cards for some ideas.

Keywords

Weather – the day-to-day condition of our atmosphere on a particular day, for example, how warm, cold, dry or wet each day is.
Climate – the average weather conditions over a longer period of time (30-50 years).

What's in the picture on the front of this card?

Photo (front): Nick Cobbing/Greenpeace

Introduction: why is the Earth getting hotter?

The Earth's 'invisible blanket'

Imagine an 'invisible blanket' of gases around the Earth. These gases trap heat in the atmosphere surrounding our planet.

This invisible blanket is not too thick, or too thin. It keeps our planet at the right temperature. On Mars the gas blanket is too thin and on Venus too thick. No life has been discovered on either planet.

Help, it's hotter than a greenhouse in here!

The Earth's gas blanket is getting thicker. This is because we are pouring more gases like carbon dioxide into the atmosphere.

These gases are also known as greenhouse gases because the gas blanket works by trapping the sun's heat in the same way as the glass walls of a greenhouse.

The problem is that the gas blanket is trapping in too much heat, making the Earth hotter. As the Earth gets hotter, we are likely to see stronger storms, and more droughts, floods and heatwaves.

Where's all the gas coming from?

Most of our energy comes from fossil fuels. These are coal, natural gas and oil. We use them to light our homes, drive our cars and heat our schools.

When we burn fossil fuels they give off carbon dioxide. We are using so much coal, oil and natural gas that too much carbon dioxide is pouring into the atmosphere.

One to remember!

Britain's schools release over five million tonnes of carbon dioxide a year. Just one tonne of carbon dioxide is enough to fill six double-decker buses!

What's in the picture on the front of this card?

Photo: Jehad Nga/Corbis/ActionAid

Drought in Kenya 2006.

Photo (front): Teresa Osorio/Greenpeace

Future world?

This map shows what scientists think could happen if the world heats up by 3-5°C.

Scientists are predicting that global temperatures will rise between 3-5°C by the end of this century if we continue as we are. This future need not happen if we act to slow climate change. Check out the *PowerDown* solutions cards.

Introduction: how is climate change affecting our world?

Learn card 3

As our world heats up, scientists predict more extreme weather such as droughts, floods or heatwaves. In many countries people say changes in the weather are already affecting their lives.

Floods in Uganda

This picture was taken in Uganda. In 2007 people experienced the worst floods in living memory. The floods were like a sea washing over the land. People went hungry because their crops were destroyed. Thousands of homes were washed away and schools closed.

"The poorest people in Africa and Asia are sending a mayday message to the rest of the world. Please help us fight climate change."

ActionAid co-ordinator, eastern Uganda 2007.

Photo: Vincent Ojumbo Wandera/ActionAid

Climate refugees in Katakwi District, Uganda 2007. Unprecedented rains caused inland seas and washed away homes and harvests.

2007: The year of weird world weather

- 23 African countries hit by worst floods in 30 years
- The world's second warmest year on record – temperatures in Greece reached 46°C!
- In England rescue services helped tens of thousands of people caught in extraordinary floods.

Drought in Kenya

This is Kaila Nampaso. He has lived through one of the worst droughts in history. A drought is a long period without rain. Like millions of others his family has gone hungry. Without rain, crops cannot grow and animals cannot graze.

Photo: ActionAid

"It's become drier and drier. Our life is on hold, waiting for clouds which promise less and less rain."

Kaila Nampaso, aged 27, from Kenya.

Climate change around the world: Mahidul's story

As the world heats up, our climate is changing. Scientists predict more extreme weather such as floods or droughts. In many countries people say changes in the weather are already affecting their lives.

Mahidul, aged 11, Bangladesh

"Hi, I'm Mahidul from Char Jattrapur. I live with my mother, who looks after our cows, my father who is too old to work and my younger brothers.

Almost every morning I go fishing. In the afternoons I sell the fish at the market – sometimes I spend all night on the river fishing. It's hard work for someone as small as me!

It never used to be like this. I used to be in Class 3 at school. My father was a carpenter. He owned a small plot of land near the Brahmaputra. The river was deep and we grew lots of crops.

Then the weather changed. Heavy rainfall flowed over the land. We also had periods of drought. The river became shallow and the land sandy and useless.

Photo: Tom Pietrasik/ActionAid

Night fishing on the Brahmaputra river, northern Bangladesh.

My family had to move over ten times to find a safe place to live. I wish I could stop being a fisher boy and go back to school."

Words to remember

Char – a small island which often gets flooded and sometimes disappears completely.
Drought – a long period without rain when crops cannot grow.
Brahmaputra – one of the longest rivers in Asia, flowing through Tibet, India and Bangladesh.

Weather watch

What's the weather like where you live? Is it changing? How do you know?

What's in the picture on the front of this card?

Photo (front): Tom Pietrasik/ActionAid

Climate change around the world: Fatima's story

Fatima lives in Assam in India. It is one of the wettest regions in the world. People say the floods here have been getting worse.

Fatima, aged 7, India

"My name is Fatima. I live in Karchua Bori village next to the Brahmaputra river. I have six brothers and sisters. Here's me at school!

Our house was badly flooded this year. To stay safe, we built two bamboo platforms inside. We put our crops on the lower platform but they got washed away.

We lived on the higher flood platform for many days. Every morning I got up at 5am to help my parents. I helped my mum boil water to drink and make tea. We had a few biscuits but were very hungry.

My younger sisters were really scared. I used to sit next to them and sing songs. One day I looked down from my platform and saw the floods getting higher. They got stronger and stronger, swirling into corners and to where we sat.

Photo: Prashant Panjiar/OnAsia/ActionAid

Fatima learning at Karchua Bori primary school, Lower Assam, India.

We had to escape to the shelters on higher ground. We shared a raft with other families. It was very wet and scary.

Now everything in my house is wet and muddy. My father can't farm the land because the waters are still lying there. The platforms must be rebuilt with new bamboos. I am learning to do this so I can help keep my family safe."

Weather words in Assamese

Flood – Banpani
Rain – Barukun
Earthquake – Bhumikampa
High speed circle winds – Ghurania Botar
Hailstone – Bardoichila

What's in the picture on the front of this card?

Photo (front): Prashant Panjiar/OnAsia/ActionAid

P

2007

Climate change around the world: Zakir's story

Storms and floods bring many dangers. In Assam, India, the floodwater can carry diseases and sometimes snakes up to four metres long!

Snake attack!

"I'm Zakir Hussain. I live with my family in Assam, India. I am seven years old.

Before the floods came I helped to build a bamboo platform in my home. When the floods came we stayed on this for ten days.

It was Friday at 8pm when a snake climbed onto our platform. It was climbing up the bamboo stilts. I was very frightened and called to my father.

I got a stick and hit the snake. It fell back into the water. It was about four metres long and it was wider than the bamboo itself.

When my father saw how I protected my family, he asked me to be on snake duty. I looked to see shadows in the water. These snakes like to glide on the top of water very fast. I beat three more snakes but none as big as the first one.

When the floods got worse, we took a small banana raft to the shelters. We saw many snakes trying to stay alive like us. My father is proud of me. He said I helped keep my family safe. Next time the floods come, I will be on snake duty again!"

Photo: Getty Images

Naja Naja: a venomous snake commonly known as the Indian Spectacled Cobra.

Surviving a snake invasion: Zakir's top tips!

- Put bells on your flood platform to warn you when a snake approaches.
- Light candles at night to watch for them – it is difficult to see them in the dark.
- Tell everyone to make a noise because snakes like it nice and quiet.

What's in the picture on the front of this card?

Photo (front): Prashant Panjiar/OnAsia/ActionAid

Climate change around the world: Biplob's story

Learn card 7

In 2007 Bangladesh was hit by the worst floods for 30 years. The floods damaged around four million homes. Many children had to leave school and look for work. Without the children's help, families simply cannot survive.

Biplob, aged 11, Bangaldesh

"My name is Biplob. I live with my relatives about eight miles from my home. I work in their grocery shop. I also go to market to buy goods to sell.

Here I am with my friends. Sometimes I get time to play with them but not long enough!

Photo: Tom Pietrasik/ActionAid

Biplop and friends in Santoshoviram village, Kurigram District.

In the evening I stay in the shop. When I have finished all my chores, I lie down on the shop floor and go to sleep.

I dream of the time when my mother was still alive. We lived on the banks of the Tista River. My father grew enough crops on our plot of land to feed everyone.

Then the floods came. Our houses and land were flooded frequently by the river. We had to move many times to other places.

My father couldn't work anymore as a farmer. We lost our mother and now all of us are living in different places. Farhad, my brother, works in a clothes factory in Dhaka and my sister Ratna works as a maidservant.

I wish I could go back to finish my studies and get a good job to help my family."

What's in the picture on the front of this card?

Photo (front): Tom Pietrasik/ActionAid

Climate change around the world: Abbas' story

Abbas lives in a small village in Assam, India. Over the years the village has seen more and more floods. The floods damage crops like rice and wash away food supplies. Families often survive by fishing in dangerous waters.

Fishing in the floods

"My name is Abbas. I'm 11 years old. I live with my family near the Brahmaputra river. I have four sisters and four brothers. I am the third oldest.

I go into the water to collect fish, even during the floods. The floods make the waters dark and muddy, and it is hard to find the fish. I swim to the shallow places. Then I put the fishing nets in the water and wait silently for the fish to come.

You have to be careful during the floods. When it is raining hard and the wind is strong the waters are too angry, and they can pull you down. Sometimes the fish are sucked down and sometimes the waters throw them into the air.

I like to go with other fisher boys to the slow waters. If the water is not too deep we ride a buffalo from my house to the boat. They are friendly animals and they look after us.

Photo: Prashant Panjiar/OnAsia/ActionAid

Abbas fishing in the Brahmaputra river near his home.

When the floods are over, the fish love to play. When they jump above the water we hear a dipping sound like 'ka-pang'! I love to hear this."

Keyword

Brahmaputra – one of the longest rivers in Asia flowing through Tibet, India and Bangladesh.

What's in the picture on the front of this card?

Photo (front): Prashant Panjiar/OnAsia/ActionAid

Climate change around the world: Sophia's story

Learn card 9

As the world heats up, our climate is changing. Scientists predict more extreme weather, like droughts. Sofia and her older brother Mata Merumbe live in Tanzania. They have been living through a terrible drought for the last two years.

No rain, no food

"I am Sofia from Tanzania. I am 13 years old. I have six brothers and we are farmers. When I grow up I would like to be a nurse so that I can treat people.

Every day I help my mother. I do the domestic chores at home. Then I go to the market to help her sell fruit.

I would love to go to school. I feel bad when I see my friends go to school and I can't. My father's cows have died because of drought, so I don't think I'll be able to go to school."

Photo: Peter Murimi/ActionAid

Sophia and her brother Mata dancing with friends.

"I am Mata Merumbe. Sofia is my only sister. When it doesn't rain for two years, there is a lot of hunger.

There was very little rain at the beginning of last year. We weren't able to harvest any maize. The drought affected our cows and goats. All the cows died and right now we have only 20 goats left.

Life is very difficult. It's just started raining a little now but hunger is still a big problem. We are getting ready to plant maize. As soon as we know the rains will last, we will plant."

Keyword

Drought – a long period without rain when crops cannot grow.

What's in the picture on the front of this card?

Photo (front): Peter Murimi/ActionAid

Climate change around the world: the Amazon rainforest story

The Amazon rainforest covers 5% of planet Earth. It stretches across eight countries in South America. It helps keep our world's climate in balance.

The 'invisible rivers' of the rainforest

The Amazon rainforest is very hot. Every day billions of litres of water vapour are released into the air through a process called evaporation. As the air moves away from the rainforest to the high mountains of the Andes, it is forced southwards, transporting the water vapour like invisible flying rivers. This eventually falls as rain not only in South America but also in places as far away as Africa!

Why rainforest trees are important for our climate

- If rainforest trees are cut down the air becomes drier. There is less rain in the forest and less water vapour joins the invisible rivers. Without these 'invisible rivers' there would be more drought in the world.
- Trees store carbon in their trunks, branches and roots. When trees are chopped down, burnt or die, they give off carbon dioxide. About one fifth of all carbon dioxide being released into the atmosphere comes from dying trees.
- If all the Amazon rainforest was destroyed, 77 billion tonnes of carbon dioxide would be released into the atmosphere.

Photo: Olavo Rufino/Greenpeace

An aerial view of a cleared area in the Amazon rainforest, Brazil.

What's in the picture on the front of this card?

Photo (front): Daniel Beltrá/Greenpeace

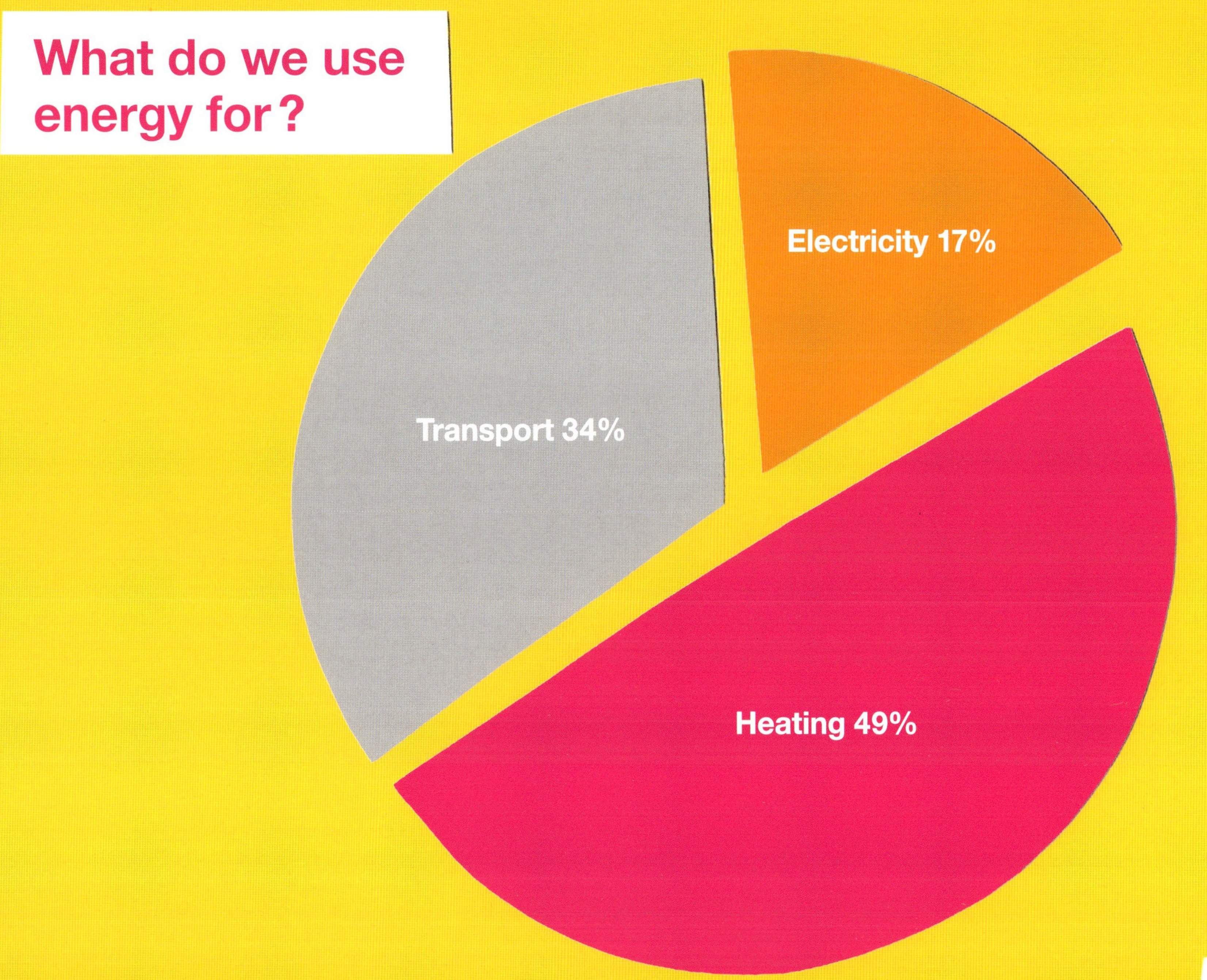

Energy use in the UK

Climate change and energy use: the big picture

We use energy to light our homes, drive our cars and heat our schools. Most of our energy comes from burning fossil fuels. These are coal, natural gas and oil.

When we burn fossil fuels they give off carbon dioxide. The amount of coal, oil and natural gas we are using is pouring too much carbon dioxide into the atmosphere.

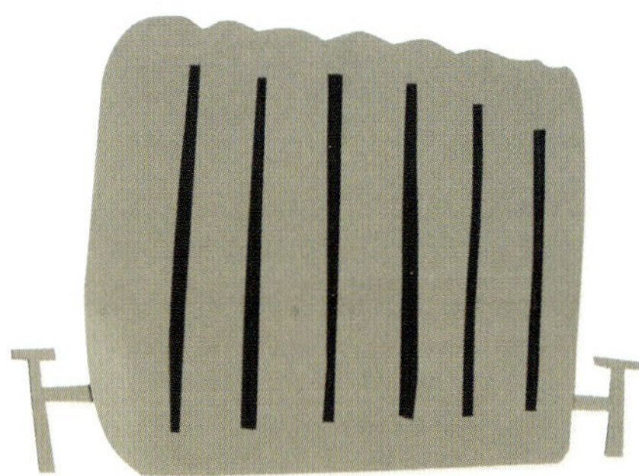

Heat for homes and schools is generated mainly using natural gas. This is found under the sea and comes from decayed plants and tiny sea creatures that lived millions of years ago. It powers things like radiators, cookers and hot water boilers. When natural gas is burnt it releases carbon dioxide.

Most forms of transport such as cars, buses or planes run on oil made into petrol or diesel. When these are burnt to give us energy they also release carbon dioxide. For example, when a car burns petrol it is able to move, but this also releases carbon dioxide through its exhaust pipe.

Electricity powers useful things like fridges, lights and washing machines. Most of our electricity comes from power stations. It is transported to our homes along cables.

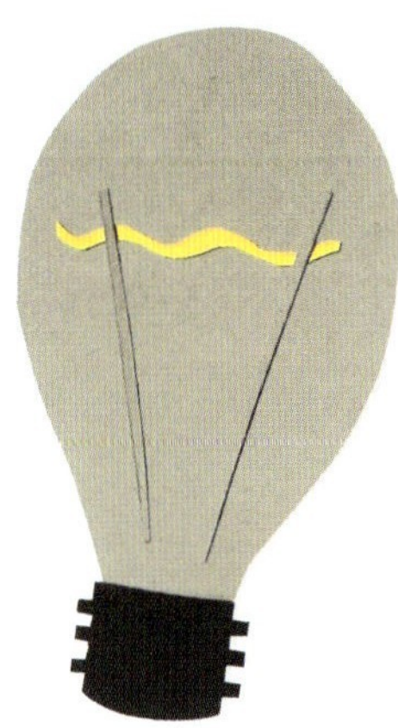

Most power stations burn coal or natural gas, which pour carbon dioxide into the atmosphere. Generating electricity in the UK produces 174 million tonnes of carbon dioxide a year.

One to remember!

The cost of energy used within all UK schools is around £350 million! Schools release over five million tonnes of carbon dioxide a year. Just one tonne of carbon dioxide is enough to fill six double-decker buses!

TERMINOLOGY
www.schoolsnet.com
.com

Climate change and energy use: electricity at school

Learn card 13

Electricity uses up a third of a school's energy but it is one of the easiest things to do something about.

Switch off at the socket!

Electrical appliances like PCs, photocopiers and interactive whiteboards gobble lots of energy when they are in 'standby' mode. Often these are only used a few hours a day but they are plugged into the wall all the time – even at weekends!

Remember your computer is not properly off unless it is switched off at the socket.

Turn off the lights

When we leave lights on in empty classrooms and corridors, we are wasting both money and energy.

Most schools use strip lights, but where you have normal light bulbs change them as traditional light bulbs waste a lot of energy: 90% of the electricity they use is wasted as heat and only 10% makes light. Changing just one light bulb to an energy-saving light bulb could save 26 kilograms of carbon dioxide a year.

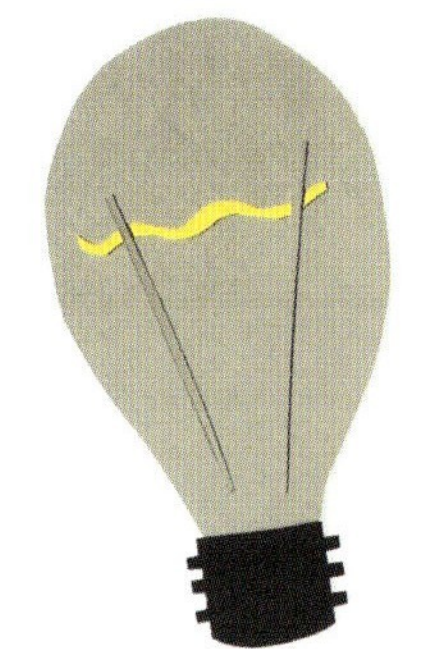

"I'm energy-hungry. I waste 90% of my energy as heat!"

"I'm energy-efficient! I last around 10 times longer than an old-fashioned light bulb."

Brain-teaser

Leaving just one computer (including peripherals and monitor) on standby when not in use can add up to £20 to the annual energy bill of a school. If a school switched off 10 computers rather than leaving them on standby, how much money could they save?
There are about 30,000 schools in the UK. If they each switched off 10 computers, how much money could be saved?

What's in the picture on the front of this card?

Photo (front): Kristian Buus/ActionAid

0.22 kW
MODE
ALARM
CLUB

Climate change and energy use: energy loss at home

Learn card 14

Homes use lots of energy to power different things. Here's a few you might know!

Home energy savers – top tips!

Switch off at the socket

In standby mode things like PCs, TVs or PlayStations gobble up energy. When you're not using them, switch them off at the socket. This will help save lots of energy as 8% of all UK energy use is from appliances left on standby!

Showers are best

Lots of energy is needed to create hot water to wash clothes, dishes and ourselves. Showers use a lot less precious energy than baths. If you've got a shower, use it!

A bright idea

Older types of light bulbs waste 90% of the electricity they use as heat. Only 10% makes light. New energy-saving light bulbs last around ten times longer than ordinary light bulbs – just one could save 26 kilograms of carbon dioxide a year.

Turn down the heat

18-20°C is an ideal room temperature. If your room thermostat is set higher than this, turn it down. If you're still cold, get moving or put more clothes on!

What's in the picture on the front of this card?

Photo (front): Kate Davison/Greenpeace

P

HG56 HLH

Climate change and energy use: transport

Learn card 15

"I run on petrol. Every time you switch on my engine I burn petrol. This releases carbon dioxide into the atmosphere. Sometimes I only carry one passenger. If my tyres are too flat I use even more petrol."

"I use lots of fuel when I take off and land. Flying in me for a short distance releases lots of CO_2 per passenger."

"Like cars, I run on petrol but I am more energy efficient because I carry more people."

"I am more energy efficient than cars or planes. I use up to 70% less energy than a plane and cause up to 85% less air pollution. I like carrying lots of people!"

"I use no petrol. I run on leg power alone. I am a good way to keep people fit and healthy."

Brain-teaser

About 30 trains and 30 planes leave London for Manchester each day. Each train produces about 35kg of CO_2 for each journey made and a plane produces about 165kg of CO_2 for each journey made. How much CO_2 is produced each day?

A plane can carry 128 passengers, and a train 384 passengers. Assuming all trains are full, how many extra trains would be needed if all flights were stopped for a day? How much CO_2 would be saved that day? How much could be saved each year if all flights between London and Manchester were stopped?

What's in the picture on the front of this card?

Photo (front): Will Rose/Greenpeace

P

This is our planet, Earth.
We only have one.

If everyone in the world used the planet's resources like the USA we would need 5.3 planets.

If everyone used them like the UK we would need 3.1 planets...

like India, 0.4 planets...

and Malawi in Africa, 0.3 planets.

Climate change solutions: global solutions

Solution card 16

The way that some of us humans are living on Earth is becoming 'unsustainable'. This means that if we carry on like this, and more people do the same, many of the world's natural resources, like forests, oil or natural gas will run out.

Worse still, it is the way we are using these resources that is leading to climate change. Countries using the most resources, like the USA, are causing the most climate change. Countries using the least resources, like Bangladesh, are suffering most from climate change.

We all share one planet – there are no other planets to move to! Our futures are connected no matter where we live. We need to work out a way of living together that does not use up the planet's precious resources, does not cause climate change and is fairer.

Finding a way to do this is called 'sustainable development'.

World leaders from countries that are causing the greatest amount of damage have the most power to make these changes happen.

World leaders – the story so far

➡ **1992. The Earth Summit in Rio, Brazil.** World leaders discussed the state of the planet and agreed to try to tackle climate change.

➡ **1997. The Kyoto Protocol.** Leaders from some of the world's richest countries agreed to reduce the amount of greenhouse gases that they are pouring into the atmosphere. Each country agreed to cut a certain amount of greenhouse gas emissions.

➡ **2005. The Kyoto Treaty.** After a lot of arguing, the Kyoto Protocol began when 170 world leaders signed this treaty! The USA would not sign it (even though it produces 25% of the world's greenhouse gas emissions).

➡ **2012. The Kyoto Protocol will need a new agreement.** World leaders have to agree what happens next.

World leader for a day

"Help! I need to cut my country's greenhouse gases. What shall I ask people to do? Mmmm. Shall I ask them, or tell them? How can I make sure they do it?"

P

NO

Climate change solutions: people power

Solution card 17

Sometimes it may feel like the world's problems are too big for us to solve. But if we work together, we can make incredible things happen.

UK climate promises

Here are some climate promises that the UK government has made:

- ➡ by the year 2020, we will reduce greenhouse gas emissions by 26-30% (compared to 1990).
- ➡ by the year 2050, we will cut carbon dioxide emissions by 60%.

Get your MP involved

MP means Member of Parliament. MPs have a real say in what the government does and can help make sure that the government keeps its promises – like the climate promises listed.

MPs are voted in by the people who live in a particular area. MPs have to listen to what their voters have to say. An MP's local area is called a constituency.

Photo: Goodshoot RF/Getty Images

The Houses of Parliament, London.

You could write a short letter to your MP either as a class or individual. You could tell your MP some of the things you have learned about climate change and the things you are doing to save energy. You could check what the government is doing to help too!

Contacting your MP is easy.
Just go to www.writetothem.com to find out who your MP is and write to them.

To find out what your MP does visit www.theyworkforyou.com

Photo (front): Nick Cobbing/Greenpeace

Vestas

Climate change solutions: Good Energy

Solution card 18

Non-renewable energy

Today, most of our energy comes from fossil fuels called natural gas, coal and oil. These are called non-renewable because one day they will run out. They also produce carbon dioxide when we burn them. Too much carbon dioxide is not good for our planet.

Renewable energy

We can also make energy from the sun, the wind, or water. It is called renewable because it can be replaced all the time and will not run out. Even better, it does not produce any carbon dioxide!

Photo: David Rose Panos/ActionAid

Pupils from St Martin at Shouldham CEVA primary school constructing and trying out a model wind turbine.

Amanda Watson from power company Good Energy tells us more:

"I work for Good Energy. We help people become part of the solution to climate change. We power over 24,000 homes, schools and businesses in the UK.
We make electricity using mostly wind power. We also use some solar power and hydro power (using moving water). Since we started we have saved a total of 196,500 tonnes of carbon dioxide. We are really proud of this!"

What form of energy am I? Am I renewable or non renewable?

"I come from the sun's rays. I can be converted into other forms of energy, like electricity. I do not release any carbon dioxide. I never run out!"

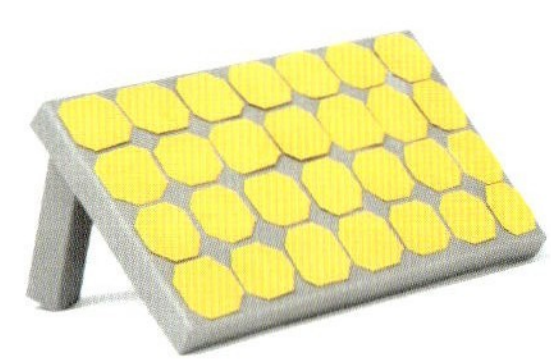

"I come from giant plants and trees buried deep in the earth millions of years ago. When you burn me I produce carbon dioxide. I will run out."

"I took millions of years to create. I come from tiny plants and animals buried deep beneath the sea bed. I have no colour or smell. I produce carbon dioxide and I will not last forever."

"I am made from moving air. When my blades turn, they connect to a generator and make electricity. The bigger I am, the more electricity I make. I will not run out."

What's in the picture on the front of this card?

Photo (front): Hu Wei/Greenpeace

School

Climate change solutions: Hamsey Green junior school, England

Solution card 19

There are lots of different ways to *PowerDown* in your school. Here are some energy saving ideas from Hamsey Green junior school pupils in Surrey. Would these work in your school? Can you think of any better ones?

School energy savers – top tips!

Switch OFF!

"There's no need for lights when it's sunny. It's already light! Also when you finish working at a computer, turn it off. Simple!"

Shut doors and windows

"Remember to close doors and windows.
If you don't then heat gets out. This is a waste of energy if you have the radiators on."

Persuade other people to *PowerDown*

"Lots of people have no idea how much energy we all waste. A good way to let parents know is through assemblies.
Writing leaflets with 'top secret' on also works because people want to read them!"

Take the walking bus

"Ever heard of a bus with no wheels, which runs on leg power?! Well, a walking bus is a way of walking to school with your friends without using any petrol. An adult leads the bus, and we get picked up at 'bus stops' along the way."

Thanks to Lauren, Year 4; Aaron, Year 5; Lauren, Holly, George, Mary, Hannah and Sam, Year 6 for these fantastic ideas.

What's in the picture on the front of this card?

Photo (front): Kristian Buus/ActionAid

Climate change solutions: Ashley Church of England primary school, England

Solution card 20

At Ashley Church of England primary school in Walton-on-Thames everyone has been working together to save energy, with some impressive results!

Pupils' top tips: how to be an energy monitor

"In every year group at school we have energy monitors checking how much energy we are using in different parts of the school. We have a software system called an ecoDriver to help us. It provides us with graphs which show us how much energy our school is using – or in the case of our solar panels, how much its producing."

Elliott, Year 6.

"We found out that Monday was the worst day because teachers needed to make photocopies for our lessons. So the energy monitors have challenged the teachers to try and photocopy less and find alternative ways to teach us!"

Nathan, Year 6.

Photo: Kristian Buus/ActionAid

Students at Ashley Church of England school, show off their ecoDriver monitor that displays live energy use in different parts of the school buildings

"Simple ecoDriver bar-graphs help us see how much energy we have used over a day or a week. We have been able to see that when we change our behaviour we save money and reduce our CO_2 emissions."

Miss Ota, class teacher.

"Since we started using ecoDriver we have made dramatic savings with our energy. Our consumption for the first three months of this year was over 50% down on last year. We had a Carbon Free Friday last week, when we tried to use as little energy as possible, and we managed to get our energy for the whole school for the day down to just 30kWhs, which is less than £3!'

Mr Dunne, headteacher.

What's in the picture on the front of this card?

Photo (front): Kristian Buus/ActionAid

Keep the heat in
Reduce waste in your bin
Help save the planet, let's save the world today
TOP TIP
Don't leave computers on stand by
How well did your class do today? Which balloon was placed on your door?
TOP TIP
Handwash dishe
TOP TIP
se products with minimum packaging

Climate change solutions: St Martin at Shouldham CEVA primary school, England

Solution card 21

Do you know how much energy your school uses to power things such as lights, computers or radiators? Any idea where most of the energy is being used up?

Here's some advice from pupils at St Martin at Shouldham CEVA primary school in Norfolk

Pupils' top tips: how to start an energy saving club

1. Choose one person from each class to be an energy-saving monitor.
2. Check each class every day (or week) at break time. Write down all the electrical equipment that has been left on or switched off.
3. Switch off equipment such as computers or lights that have been left on.
4. Put a green, orange or red balloon outside each class.

Green

"Well done, you've switched everything off and closed the doors."

Orange

"Not bad, you've switched some things off."

Red

"Warning! You've left PCs on, and heat is escaping from the windows."

Teachers' top tips: getting solar power at your school

Solar energy comes from the sun's rays that reach the Earth. Solar energy can be converted into other forms of energy, like electricity.
Headteacher Marika Mears explains how it works. "We have solar panels on our roof. Even on a cloudy day, they convert daylight into electricity. The electricity helps light our classrooms, power our computers, even cook our dinners!

The electricity produces no carbon dioxide and it is cheap. We are saving six tonnes of carbon dioxide a year and over £1,000 a year off our electricity bills, which is just over half our total bill at today's prices. We will even sell some back to the National Grid during the summer months."

What's in the picture on the front of this card?

Photo (front): David Rose Panos/ActionAid

P

Solution card 22

Climate change solutions: Karchua Bori primary school, India

Cutting the level of greenhouse gases we produce is the most important thing we can do. We are also going to have to work out ways of living or adapting to climate change.

Here is what is happening in India, where climate change is likely to have some of the worst effects.

"*Namaste!* My name is Imrana. I'm 11 years old. My school keeps getting flooded. One year the water was so fierce that our whole school was destroyed. When a flood comes it is good to be prepared. Here are some of the things we've been learning to do."

Photo: Prashant Panjiar/OnAsia/ActionAid

A hazard map created by pupils at Karchua Bori primary school, Assam, India. Pupils use the map to investigate which parts of their school are most at risk and what they can do to protect it.

Top tips: flood survival at school

Find the flood platform

Don't let the water rise above your head, get to the flood platform quickly! It is high off the ground, so it is the safest place to go.

Learn to swim

Flood water can rise quickly. It turns black and moves in fierce circles. Learning to swim is very important. Older children can help teach younger children and make it fun!

Make a lifesaver

When the floods are strong, they can pull you under. Use bottles and jerry cans to make a life jacket. This will help you float. You can also make a canoe using banana plants, bamboo and tarpaulin.

Be a life saver

Lots of people hold onto trees in a flood. Sometimes they get injuries like broken arms and legs. Learn how to help someone by practising first aid on your friends.

Plant trees

Plant a few trees between your school and any water nearby. This could be a river or lake. The trees will stop the force of the waters and protect you more.

What's in the picture on the front of this card?

Photo (front): Prashant Panjiar/OnAsia/ActionAid